NATIONAL GEOGRAPHIC

T0042359

What Plant Is This?

Leroy Taylor

What plant is this?

It has **stalks**.

It has **leaves**.

It has **flowers**.

It has fruit.

It is a banana plant.

Yum!

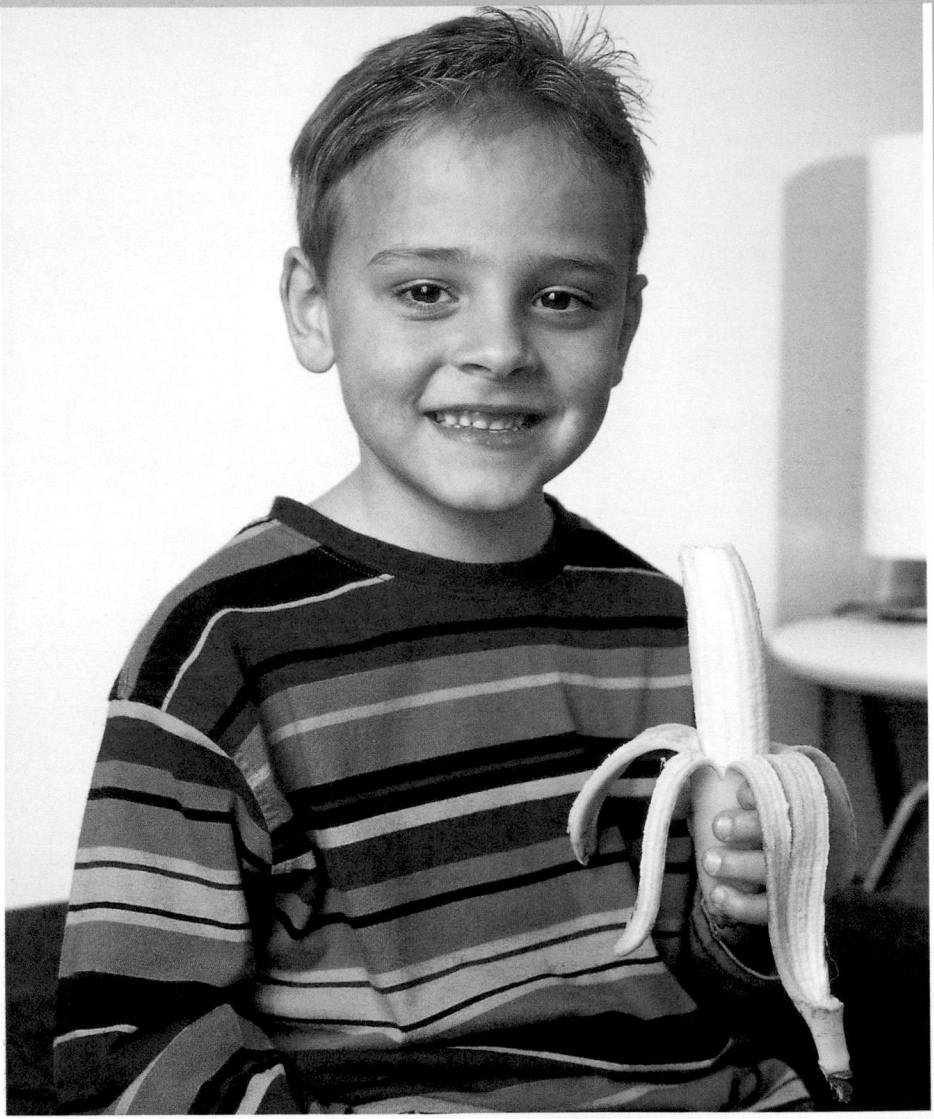